Jump into Fiction

By the Campfire

The sun has set.
The campfire burns hot.
It is time for a story.

Park Rangers

STEAMBOAT
GEYSER

Rachael Dupree

Rangers at the Park

Take a hike at a national park.
You may see a park ranger there!

Ranger Sally tells a story.
The stars twinkle.
The fire glows.
It is a good story!

Back to Nonfiction

Roving Rangers

Follow the ranger through the parks.
What do you see?

Mount Rainier

Yellowstone

Mount Rushmore

Redwood

Great Sand Dunes

Grand Canyon

Carlsbad Caverns

Waco Mammoth

The Oldest National Park

Yellowstone National Park was
the first national park.
It became one in 1872.

There are tall trees and big mountains.
There are deep canyons and wildlife.

Acadia

Mammoth Cave

Congaree

Great Smoky Mountains

Everglades

This map shows some national parks.

Park rangers work at national parks. They keep the parks and people safe. They take care of nature's special places.

Think and Talk

What can you learn about rangers from this picture?

Park rangers are easy to find.
Just look for their uniforms and badges!

Wear It Well

The ranger badge has changed over time. It now shows a bison in a national park.

Taking Care

Park rangers love nature.

They want other people to love it too!

They also want everyone to stay safe and follow the rules.

Think and Talk

How are park rangers
and teachers alike?

Park rangers show people the best sites to visit.
If someone gets lost or hurt, park rangers are there to help.

Bark Rangers

Some dogs work at national parks.
They help keep people safe.
They are called "bark rangers."

People can ask park rangers questions.
Park rangers know a lot about their parks.

Ranger You

You can practice being a park ranger!

Go outside.

Study the rocks, dirt, trees, and bugs.

Junior Ranger

You can sign up to be a Junior Ranger. You will learn more about the parks. You can earn your very own badge too!

Share what you find with a friend.
Teach them what you know.
You are now like a park ranger!

Civics in Action

One job park rangers do is to teach people about nature. They are experts! You can be an expert too.

1. Pick something in nature you really like. It might be a plant or a tree. It might be a mountain or a river near you.

2. Ask a grown-up you know to help you learn about it. Look online. Read books about it.

3. Draw or paint a picture of it.

4. Invite your family to your ranger talk. Show them the picture. Tell them what you learned.